Contents

Ready for take-off

It's 6:00 am. My alarm goes off! It's time to wake up and make my way from the hotel to the airport.

As the Captain working for an international airline, I often stay in hotels abroad. Today, I'm flying a Boeing 747 jumbo jet from Bangkok back to London. We're scheduled to leave at 9:30 am. I will need to be at the airport by 8:30 am to complete all my pre-flight checks.

Bangkok airport is huge.

I did a bit of sightseeing on my Bangkok stopover. The Grand Palace was amazing.

I catch a minibus from the hotel with a group of flight attendants and another pilot. We all work for the same airline. It's a humid, foggy morning in Bangkok, and the traffic is slow. We arrive at the airport just in time.

Bumper to bumper on my way to the airport – come on, I've got a plane to fly!

The check-in area is packed as we make our way to the crew area. I meet my First Officer, and we go over the flight plan for the journey. We check altitudes and look at predicted weather patterns. We examine the route we are going to take and calculate the fuel needed.

Sandy, the check-in assistant, is always friendly and helpful.

I grab a coffee with the First Officer and flight crew before we head for the plane. Once in the cockpit, I check the logbook to see if there were any problems with the plane during its previous flight. I also check the flight controls. When all the passengers have boarded the aircraft, the First Officer and I prepare for take-off.

loading the luggage

DIDYOUKNOW?

Thirsty plane
A Boeing 747 uses around 12,000 litres of fuel in its take-off and climb.

ready for take-off

I'm given the go-ahead

The First Officer is second in command and sits on the right-hand side of the cockpit. He or she has the same level of training as the Captain. Safety is the main reason for having two pilots on a flight. The First Officer helps with flying and gives a second opinion on pilot decisions. This reduces the chance of pilot error.

As we taxi to the runway, the Air Traffic Controller makes contact through my headset. They let me know the runway is clear. We are ready for take-off! The First Officer takes his foot off the brake pedals, and the plane heads down the runway.

"V1", calls the First Officer. This stands for Velocity 1. It is the speed at which we can still abandon the take-off if something goes wrong. Within seconds, we are travelling at over 200 km/hour. I pull the control column towards me, and the plane's nose lifts into the air.

I pull back a little further, and the front wheels leave the ground. I pull back even further, and the plane leaves the ground completely.

"V2", calls the First Officer as the plane reaches Velocity 2. This is the speed at which we need to be travelling to climb higher into the air. I pull right back on the control column, and the plane soars. As the plane climbs, I bank left to stay on our flight path. At around 10,000 metres, I push the control column forward to level out the plane. We're on our way to London! It's time to address the passengers, "Good morning everyone. This is Captain Thomas Morgan speaking …".

Tow-cars – sometimes large planes need a bit of help manoeuvring into position.

How I became a commercial pilot

I've always been fascinated with planes and flying. When I was a child my father used to take me to air shows. I loved the old planes and learnt all their names.

I always wanted to fly!

Going to airshows was so exciting.

When I turned 16, I got a flying lesson for my birthday. From then on, I was hooked. I read everything I could about planes and joined the ATC (Air Training Corps).

Fantastic birthday present!

At school I gained good A-levels in maths, physics and geography. I then went to university to do a degree in Aviation Technology.

Pilot training was provided on this specialist course and I got my Private Pilot Licence (PPL).

After university I was really lucky to get an airline sponsorship to work towards my Airline Transport Pilot Licence (ATPL). At first I worked as a co-pilot with a 'frozen' ATPL to get the hours of flying experience.

Some years later, as a second officer I had to do 50 flights supervised by an experienced training captain. Eventually I became a full first officer flying with a line captain. I still had to do a further 1,500 hours flying before I obtained the full ATPL.

A pilot's life

Being a commercial pilot is exciting, but also hard work.

- Working hours depend on your destination, and flight preparation time. For example, flying to Sydney or Los Angeles, means you'll be working very long hours.
- Sleeping patterns are sometimes irregular, and jet lag may affect your health.
- Days off depend on the length of your flight. Pilots may also receive free airfares to their holiday destinations.
- Long flights mean time spent away from family and friends.
- Visiting many parts of the world is a definite bonus.
- Wages are good. Co-pilots can earn between £21,000 and £43,000 a year, depending on experience. Captains can earn between £55,000 and £80,000 a year.

9

DIFFERENT KINDS OF PILOTS

There are many different kinds of pilots. Some pilots fly professionally and others fly just for fun. Each kind of pilot has a different qualification.

Here are the four basic types of pilot licences, from the least to the most qualified:

- student pilot licence
- private pilot licence
- commercial pilot (CPL) licence
- air transport pilot (ATPL) licence

approaching the runway

DIDYOUKNOW?

Pilots are restricted to 900 flying hours per year.

Usually pilots work in pairs, but on some long-haul flights there may be four pilots. They are employed in:

- passenger scheduled services
- passenger charter services
- freight services
- general aviation – private aircraft, flying schools, and companies transporting workers to oil and gas rigs.

Pilot Stripes

The number of stripes on the sleeves of uniform jackets, and on the shoulders of a uniform shirt, indicate the following ranks:

4 Stripes = Captain
3 Stripes = First Officer
2 Stripes = Second Officer

Pilots can also train for additional qualifications such as:
- flying special types of aircraft, e.g. seaplanes
- instrument rating, e.g. flying in cloud or at night
- certified flight instruction, e.g. teaching others to fly
- aerobatic flying, e.g. learning to do loop-the-loops.

People learn to fly through the military as well, but their licensing system differs from the civilian one. The Air Force, Army and Navy all have aircraft as part of their firepower.

CPL vs ATPL

You need a Commercial Pilot Licence (CPL) to earn an income from flying aircraft. With a CPL, you can fly charters, scenic flights and low capacity airlines. You need an Air Transport Pilot Licence (ATPL) to fly aircraft that require two pilots, a multi-crew aircraft, for example. This includes all jet airliners and aircraft such as the Qantas Link propeller aeroplanes.

Good eyesight and fitness needed

To qualify for a commercial pilot licence, you have to take the tests set by the European Aviation Safety Agency (see page 45). The use of corrective lenses is not a problem as long as the corrected vision is adequate. You cannot be colour blind or deaf. Some airlines impose height and weight restrictions and you must pass a strict medical examination. Information on all medical requirements can be found on the CAA website: www.caa.co.uk.

GET YOUR EYES TESTED

Student pilots

This is where everyone starts. Pilot training varies depending on the type of pilot licence. While training, flying privileges are limited. Students are introduced to the basics of flying, including airport-to-airport and cross-country flying skills, and interaction with Air Traffic Control. Student pilots must complete all their flights with a flight instructor on board. A student pilot can only fly solo once they:

- are over the age of 16
- have passed medical testing
- have mastered the basic skills and study topics of flight
- have received their instructor's sign-off.

Private pilots

Private pilots are the largest group of pilots. They must be at least 17 years of age and have a minimum of 40 hours' flight experience. This includes:

- 5 hours of general flight time as the pilot in command
- 5 hours of cross-country flight time as the pilot in command
- 2 hours of instrument flight time, i.e. flying only with reference to aircraft instruments.

a helicopter pilot

a private jet aircraft

a luxury private jet interior

12

Commercial pilots

Commercial pilots are paid to fly aircraft. In the UK, they are usually between 18 and 24 and individual airlines have height restrictions between 5 ft 2 in (1.57 metres) and 6 ft 3 in (1.90 metres).
You also need to prove you have:

- great communication skills
- self-confidence and a clear speaking voice
- level-headedness, calmness and the ability to think and act quickly
- logical problem-solving skills
- team-work and motivating skills
- a responsible attitude and good concentration
- intelligence and emotional stability.

You can fund your own training at a Civil Aviation Authority (CAA)-approved training school, but you would have to pay the full cost of the course (around £50,000 to £60,000 in total). You can get a complete list of training providers from British Airline Pilots Association (BALPA). Alternatively, you may be lucky enough to get a sponsorship with an airline, or train with the forces (see page 43 for more details).

piloting a small plane

Who's who?

The pilot in command is called the Captain. They sit on the left-hand side of the cockpit. He or she is in charge of making major command decisions, leading the crew team, managing emergencies and handling troublesome passengers.

Time to refuel — this turbo-prop is much smaller than the Airbus A380.

Different types of aircraft

There are many different kinds of aircraft, such as microlights, helicopters, light aircraft and military aircraft. Aeroplanes carry passengers, freight and sometimes weapons.

Microlights

Microlights are simple planes. They are similar to hang-gliders, with a small engine attached and they can carry up to two people.

Light aircraft

Light aircraft are small planes usually with a single engine. Some can carry three to four passengers. Light aircraft can take-off and land in small airfields.

Hot air ballons

Commercial hot air balloon pilots must have a commercial pilot licence.

Business jets

Business jets are small planes, owned or hired by large companies.

Seaplanes

Seaplanes are fitted with special floats, so they can land on water.

Cargo carriers

Cargo carriers transport goods to all parts of the world. With some carriers, the tail can swing aside or the nose can swing open for easy loading.

Jumbo jets

Jumbo jets, like the Boeing 747, can fly long distances. They hold around 400 passengers, and fly all around the world.

Military aircraft

Military-transport planes carry weapons, large numbers of troops and equipment, such as tanks and trucks. Air-combat planes carry out reconnaissance missions or attacks on enemy forces.

The history of flight

More than 700 years ago, the Chinese invented the first kites. This started humans thinking about flying. Kites are important to the history of flight as they were the forerunner to balloons and gliders.

Chinese kite circa 1800

Ideas take flight

More than 500 years ago, the Italian artist and inventor Leonardo da Vinci drew designs for flying machines. His Ornithopter flying machine demonstrated how man could fly. The modern day helicopter is based on this concept. His theories about flight were correct, but at the time there wasn't an engine powerful enough to make his machines work.

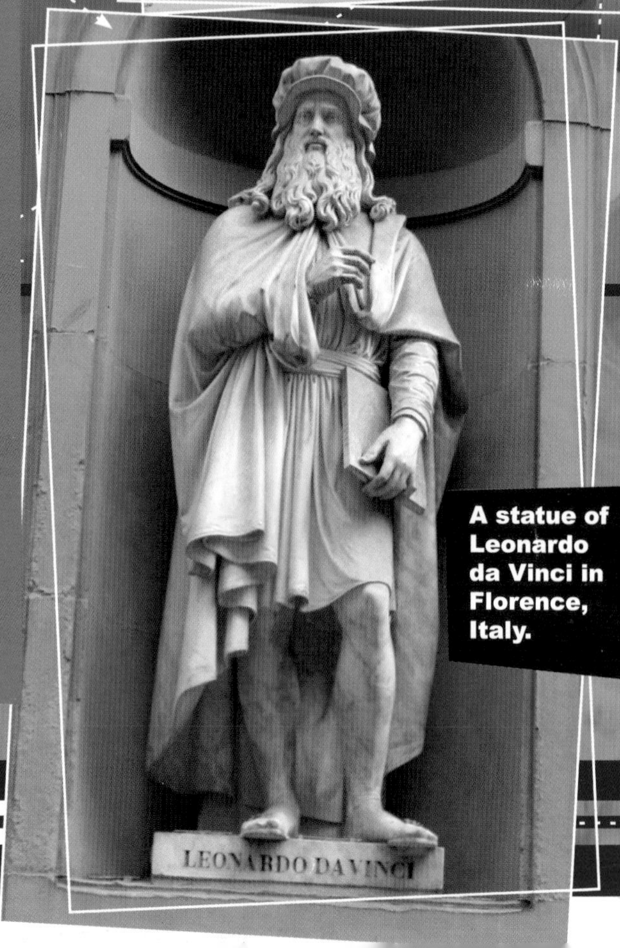

A statue of Leonardo da Vinci in Florence, Italy.

LEONARDO DA VINCI

In the 1880s, the petrol engine was invented. This made it possible to fly aircraft powered by an engine. In 1903, the Wright brothers, Wilbur and Orville, made the world's first powered, controlled and sustained flight in the aircraft, *Flyer 1*. Orville Wright flew the plane for 36 metres, approximately 3 metres off the ground. After they made improvements to the aircraft, the Wright brothers flew for around an hour. Within six years, pilots in France and the USA began using the Wright aircraft designs.

The Wright brothers' aeroplane, *Flyer 1*, is in the Smithsonian Institute, Washington DC.

The magnetic compass

The magnetic compass links all forms of aeronautical navigation. Almost every type of plane has a simple magnetic compass mounted to the windshield of the instrument panel. It is extremely reliable as it uses no power or advanced technology. Every airway and runway is numbered according to its magnetic or compass orientation.

A drawing of Wilbur Wright and *Flyer 1*.

Flight
TIMELINE

a World War I aeroplane

1903 — Orville Wright makes the first sustained, powered flight lasting 12 seconds. Later that day, Wilbur Wright flew for 59 seconds.

1937 — The jet engine was built by British engineer Frank Whittle.

1939 — Russian-American engineer Igor Sikorsky designed the first successful helicopter.

1947 — The first aircraft flew at supersonic speed in the USA.

1949 — The De Havilland Comet, the first commercial airliner, entered service in the UK.

1970 — The Boeing 747 jumbo jet was launched.

1976 — The world's first supersonic commercial airliner, Concorde, made its first scheduled flight from London to Washington.

2006 — The largest commercial aircraft, the Airbus A380's first commercial flight from Singapore to Sydney.

2010 — Virgin Galactic hopes to launch the world's first commercial flights into space.

a World War II aeroplane

Aeroplanes have changed a lot since the olden days!

Famous PILOTS

LOUIS BLERIOT

The Frenchman, Louis Bleriot, designed and built a series of planes. In 1909, he became the first person to fly across the English Channel. At an average speed of 60 km/hour, the journey took approximately 37 minutes. Bleriot reported that he had to wrestle the controls constantly to keep his monoplane steady.

An artist's impression of Louis Bleriot's flight across the English Channel.

CHARLES LINDBERGH

In 1927, American Charles Lindbergh was the first person to fly solo, non-stop across the Atlantic Ocean. It took him 33 hours and 39 minutes to fly 5,800 km from New York to Paris in his monoplane, *the Spirit of St Louis*. His average speed for the flight was 173 km/hour.

Charles Lindbergh, in front of the Spirit of St Louis.

Many modern fighter jets are supersonic.

Famous PILOTS

Some people still love flying in vintage planes!

CHARLES KINGSFORD SMITH AND CHARLES ULM

Charles Kingsford Smith and his co-pilot Charles Ulm were famous Australian pilots who set many flying records. In 1928, they became the first pilots to fly across the Pacific Ocean. Their flight from San Francisco to Brisbane took nine and a half days.

Charles Kingsford Smith before his last flight. He disappeared over Calcutta in 1935.

Air shows often display antique aircraft.

Famous
PILOTS

Amelia Earhart

AMELIA EARHART

Amelia Earhart was an American pilot who became famous for her daring, long-distance flights. In 1932, flying her *Lockhead Vega* plane, she became the first woman to fly solo across the Atlantic Ocean. In 1935, she was the first woman to fly from Hawaii to California. Amelia Earhart's success encouraged many women to take up flying.

Trip 1

Trip 2

Trip 3

Trip 4

DIDYOUKNOW?

Plane vs Car
There is enough fuel in a full tank of a Jumbo jet to drive an average car four times around the world.

FORCES AND FLIGHT

When an aircraft is airborne, four forces are at work – lift, weight, thrust and drag. Aeroplanes need engine power to provide thrust, pushing the aircraft forward. Friction against the rushing air produces drag.

Drag slows the movement of the aircraft. Lift from under the wings holds the aeroplane up, and the weight of the aeroplane pulls it down. When an aeroplane is in the air, and all four forces are in balance, the aircraft flies straight and at a steady speed.

UP, UP AND AWAY!

You need a lot of lift to keep a 396,893 kg Boeing 747 jumbo in the air — that's why it has such massive wings. The total area of a 747's wings is 525 m². That's big enough to fit around 45 cars!

Jumbo jet wings — the size of a small car park!

the airbus A380

Nicknamed the *Super Jumbo*, the Airbus A380 is the length of eight buses and has enough room on its massive wings to park 70 cars. It made its first commercial flight on the 25 October 2007 from Singapore to Sydney.

Wings

An aeroplane's wings have an *aerofoil* shape. This means the top surface of the wing is more curved than the lower surface. The aerofoil shape means that air flows faster above the wing than below it. The faster moving air sucks the wing upward, creating an upward force called *lift*.

a sunset landing

boomerang wing

DIDYOUKNOW?

Boomerang
A bent aerofoil wing can be called a boomerang!

23

CONTROL SURFACES

Control surfaces are the moving parts of the aircraft. They make the plane climb, descend and turn in flight.

There are three main control surfaces.

1 The rudder on the tail fin moves the plane's nose left or right and keeps the plane balanced.

2 Nose elevators on the tail lift the nose up or down.

3 Ailerons on the wings control the direction of the roll or *bank* of the plane.

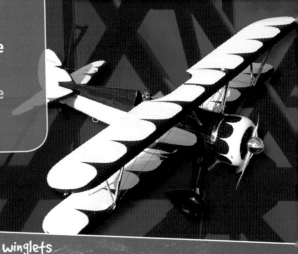

winglets

virginblue.com.au

Virgin

VH-VOL

Ailerons and spoilers

Pilots change the shape of the wings during take-off and landing to control *lift*. Increasing the size of the wing, and flying at a lower speed, reduces lift. This makes it possible for the aircraft to descend. Modern commercial aircraft have *winglets*. They help reduce drag and improve fuel efficiency.

The pilot moves these panels to control the plane's movement.

Hinged surfaces are called ailerons.

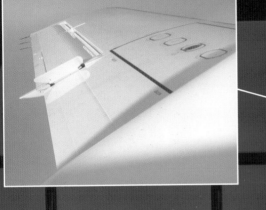

Pilots change the wing shape using ailerons and spoilers. Ailerons give the aircraft roll control. Aileron is a French word that means *little wing*. They are hinged surfaces on the very outer edge of aircraft wings. Unlike spoilers, ailerons are always used together so that when one goes up, the other goes down.

Spoilers are wing panels that control lift and assist in roll control. They are installed on the top surface of the wing. When used together, they reduce lift. Panels extend from the wing, helping the aircraft to slow down and descend. They spoil the lifting ability of the wing, hence the name *spoilers*. The pilot can also extend them one at a time to cause roll.

Spoilers reduce an aeroplane's lift.

Aircraft controls

Here are a number of standard controls found in an aircraft.

CONTROL COLUMN
The control column controls the steering of the aircraft. It is connected to ailerons on the wings and elevator panels on the tail. Pilots use the column to control climbing, diving, and banking left or right.

The rudder balances the aircraft.

THROTTLE
The throttle adjusts the thrust that the engines produce.

RUDDER PEDALS
Rudder pedals control the rudder. The rudder balances the aircraft while turning, or when strong winds move the aircraft about.

BRAKES
Brakes stop the aircraft and control how it turns once it is on the ground. Aircraft may also have a parking brake to stop it rolling when parked.

Brakes control how a plane turns on the ground.

Spoiler levers control flaps on the wings.

SPOILER LEVERS
These control the spoilers on the wings, especially when landing.

TRIM CONTROLS
These are usually knobs that adjust pitch or roll.

AUTOPILOT
Large, complex aircraft have autopilot controls. The autopilot system is part of an aircraft's electronic equipment. Autopilot controls are used to maintain altitude, climb, descend or turn – anything that a human pilot can do! They are very useful on long flights so that pilots can take a break.

The pilot controls the plane. Autopilot controls can do this too.

BUILT TO WITHSTAND A STORM
Planes are built to take a remarkable amount of force so they won't fall apart in a storm. Their wings are slightly flexible to reduce the effect of turbulence on board the aircraft.

27

Aircraft Instruments

Aircraft have instruments to provide the pilot with important information.

Basic aircraft instruments include:
- airspeed indicator – indicates how fast the plane is moving through the air
- altimeter – indicates the altitude of the aircraft, above the ground or above sea level
- attitude indicator – also called an artificial horizon, indicates the exact orientation of the plane as it pitches and rolls through the air.

Modern aeroplanes have lots of instruments to keep track of.

Keeping yourself the right way up – even when you can't see anything!

Most aircraft also have these instruments:
- turn coordinator – helps the pilot to maintain control while turning the aircraft
- rate-of-climb indicator – shows the rate at which the aircraft is climbing or descending
- engine instruments – show the status of each aircraft engine, e.g. the operating speed, thrust and temperature
- navigation and flight plan displays – help pilots stay on course
- weather radar displays – indicate oncoming weather conditions.

Faster than a speeding rocket?

Not quite! Aeroplanes are the second fastest flying machines after rockets. Commercial, jet aircraft can reach speeds of up to 900 km/hour. In contrast, supersonic aircraft, such as modern fighter jets, can travel faster than the speed of sound – over 1,230 km/hour!

NAVIGATION INSTRUMENTS

Navigation instruments help aircraft fly above the clouds, without any visual points of reference.

Older planes had fewer cockpit instruments.

Planes follow set routes from airport to airport. Radio signals from beacons, which are hundreds of kilometres apart, identify these routes. Each beacon has its own signal, and aeroplanes tune into the signal like tuning into a radio station.

Until recently, pilots used a radio magnetic indicator to navigate. These days, Inertial Reference Systems and Global Positioning Systems (GPS) help aircraft to fly more efficient, direct routes. The Inertial Reference Systems are onboard gyroscopes that determine the aircraft's position as it flies.

Radio signal beacon – looks more like a space ship!

29

FLIGHTPLANNING

Planning a flight involves two critical safety aspects.
1 Calculating the amount of fuel the aeroplane
  needs to reach its destination.
2 Ensuring a safe route to
  avoid collision.

Flight planning depends on accurate weather forecasts. Strong head and tail winds, and changes in air temperature, affect how much fuel a plane consumes. Safety regulations require planes to carry more than the minimum amount of fuel needed.

It's helpful knowing ahead of time what you'll be flying into!

A pilot sends the flight plan to the control tower around 30 minutes before departure.

DESTINATION CHANGE
A flight plan usually has an alternative departure and destination airport in case of unforeseen circumstances such as bad weather.

Some of these Air Traffic Control towers look like they're from Star Wars!

FLIGHT-MANAGEMENT SYSTEMS

Modern commercial aircraft use internal flight-management systems. These computer systems monitor information such as flight routes, aircraft speed, engine settings and estimated times of arrival. They update the aircraft's flight plan throughout the flight.

A commercial flight plan includes:
1 airline name and flight number
2 type of aircraft and equipment
3 intended airspeed and cruising altitude
4 route of flight, including the departure and destination airport.

DIDYOUKNOW?

Air safety
Most accidents that occur during a turbulent flight are caused by passengers not wearing seatbelts.

The majority of commercial airline pilots are men, but a few women are now entering this competitive career.

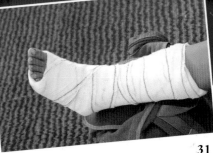

FLIGHTPLANNING

Once the air traffic controllers in the control tower have the flight-plan information, they generate a flight progress report from a computer. This will pass from controller to controller throughout the plane's flight. The report is constantly updated and contains all the necessary data to track the plane during its flight.

A world-wide chain — flight progress reports pass from controller to controller.

Most commercial planes travel between different airports. Private aircraft, commercial sightseeing tours and military planes may land at the same airport they took off from. These are known as circular or out-and-back flights.

Sky motorways
Planes follow routes called *airways*. These are like a plane's personal road and prevent mid-flight collisions. Airways are separated vertically by 305 to 610 m.

an aeroplane banking

U-TURN IN A PLANE
Planes do not turn — they bank or lean in whichever direction the pilot steers. For example, to bank left the pilot moves the control column left. This makes the ailerons on the left wing tilt up, pushing the wing down. The ailerons on the right wing tilt down, pushing the wing up.

DIDYOUKNOW?
Speedier than sound
Concorde was the only commercial aircraft faster than the speed of sound. It ceased flights in 2003 due to safety concerns.

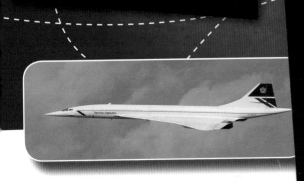

33

COMMUNICATION

Pilots use special code words to communicate with fellow pilots and control towers. The NATO Phonetic Alphabet assigns code words to the letters of the English alphabet. NATO stands for North Atlantic Treaty Organisation. Correct pronunciation of the words over radio or telephone is vital.

Roger that, Air Traffic control

The NATO Phonetic Alphabet

LETTER	CODE WORD	PRONUNCIATION
A	Alfa	AL FAH
B	Bravo	BRAH VOE
C	Charlie	CHAR LEE
D	Delta	DELL TAH
E	Echo	ECK OH
F	Foxtrot	FOKS TROT
G	Golf	GOLF
H	Hotel	HO TELL
I	India	IN DEE AH
J	Juliet	JEW LEE ETT
K	Kilo	KEY LOH
L	Lima	LEE MAH
M	Mike	MIKE
N	November	NO VEM BER
O	Oscar	OSS CAH
P	Papa	PAH PAH
Q	Quebec	KEH BECK
R	Romeo	ROW ME OH
S	Sierra	SEE AIR RAH
T	Tango	TANG GO
U	Uniform	YOU NEE FORM
V	Victor	VIK TAH
W	Whisky	WISS KEY
X	X-ray	EX RAY
Y	Yankee	YANK KEY
Z	Zulu	ZOO LOO

CALL SIGNS

International aircraft have registration numbers, just like a car. It is a country prefix and a series of letters and numbers. For example, a plane registered as N9876T would use the call sign, *November, niner eight seven six tango.*

Jumbos are expensive!

Pricey planes
The A380 Airbus costs about £152 million each. The smaller Boeing 747–400 costs about £121 million.

Learn the lingo

PILOT SPEAK	MEANING
Affirmative	Yes
Negative	No
Mayday	Emergency Help
Roger	Message received
ETA	Estimated time of arrival
ETD	Estimated time of departure

A380 vs 747

As of 2006, the Airbus A380 is now officially the largest commercial airliner in the world. It is 15 m wider, 4 m taller, 2 m longer and 118 tonnes heavier than the Boeing 747. The A380 even has space for cocktail bars, billiard rooms, showers, libraries, and sleeping quarters tucked under the floorboards for staff. With a 79.8 m wingspan, it is too large for most airport docking bays.

READING THE WEATHER

Pilots must constantly keep an eye on weather conditions. Weather radars, in a plane's nose, beam radio signals at clouds. The signals bounce back and let the pilot know how big and close the clouds are.

Wild weather ahead – but how close is it?

Turbulence

Storm clouds also appear on a plane's navigation display. Rough conditions inside clouds are called turbulence. Turbulence occurs when there are gusty, unpredictable air currents. It often occurs unexpectedly.

Turbulence during mealtime is the worst!

Gusty air currents are sometimes unexpected.

A number of different weather conditions cause turbulence. The most common is a thunderstorm. Flying through a patch of cloud will often jostle the aircraft. Turbulence is also caused by flying over mountains, near jet streams at high altitude, near a frontal system, or where there are temperature changes in the air.

Turbulence may also occur when the sky is clear of clouds. This is called clear-air turbulence or CAT. CAT occurs when a plane flies from a slow-moving air mass of about 19–37 km/hour, into or near a jet stream moving at more than 185 km/hour. CAT doesn't appear on the radar, but flight-plan forecasts warn pilots of possible turbulence ahead.

DIDYOUKNOW?

Fear of flying
Turbulence is one of main reasons why people are afraid to fly.

WORRYING WEATHER

Fliers overestimate the effects of turbulence — what passengers might consider a very bumpy ride, will only appear as a slight jiggle on the cockpit altimeter. Pilots avoid unstable air if possible, so their passengers feel more comfortable. But weather reports aren't always reliable. Most of the time, the pilot and crew know all they can do is sit back and wait for the gusty winds to pass.

DIDYOUKNOW?

Your chances of being involved in an aircraft accident are about 1 in 11 million. On the other hand, your chances of being killed in an automobile accident are 1 in 5000. Statistically, you are at far greater risk driving to the airport than getting on an aeroplane.

Happy customers are our top priority!

BLACKBOXES

If a plane crashes, it's important to work out what went wrong. Planes carry a device called a *black box*. Black boxes contain a flight-data recorder and a cockpit voice recorder. They record vital information on a plane prior to an accident. Black boxes are built to withstand extreme heat, violent crashes and enormous amounts of pressure. They are often the only devices left intact after an airline accident. Black boxes provide investigators with clues as to why a plane crashed.

Black boxes record cabin temperature and the outside temperature.

Black boxes contain the following data —
- time
- altitude
- air pressure
- airspeed
- vertical acceleration
- magnetic heading
- control column position
- rudder pedal position
- control wheel position
- fuel flow
- horizontal stabiliser

Planes are fitted with sensors that gather data. These sensors monitor acceleration, airspeed, altitude, wing-flap settings, outside temperature, cabin temperature and pressure, and engine performance. All the sensor data is collected and sent to the aircraft's flight-data acquisition unit. It transmits information from the sensors to the black boxes.

Bright orange

The black box is actually coloured bright orange. This is to make it easy to find. It is called black because the box is often retrieved after a serious accident where people have died, or in other words a black event.

FLIGHT RECORDER DO NOT OPEN

AC AMPERS

LINE IN

AUXILIARY

FLIGHT RECORDER
Serial No.
Model No.
Issue Date
Service Date

Cockpit voice recorders

Microphones built into the plane's cockpit record conversations of the flight crew. They also pick up any ambient noise in the cockpit, such as knocks and thuds.

Microphones are built into the plane's cockpit.

Preparing to land

As we fly out of the storm cloud, I contact London Heathrow Air Traffic Control.

I push the control column forward. The altimeter indicator shows I am flying at the height requested by Air Traffic Control. I then pull back on the column to level out the plane. Adjusting the wing spoilers to reduce the lift, we continue our descent and approach the runway.

Around 8 km from the airport, the primary flight display picks up two signals from the runway. These signals help guide us onto land. One of them gives me the correct angle of our descent. The other helps me to keep in line with the centre of the runway.

TOUCHDOWN

I slow the plane's speed, and pull the wing-flap lever down. This increases the wings' edges so we can fly at a slower speed. The runway rushes towards us. The First Officer pulls a lever to lower the plane's wheels.

I pull the control column back, and the plane's nose tips up. I reduce the engine power, and the plane touches down on the runway.

I put the engines into reverse, slowing down our forward movement. Now, instead of thrust coming out of the back of the engine it shoots forward out of the vents. At the same time, the wheel brakes come on and we gently roll to a halt. We then steer the plane towards our designated arrival gate.

PINK BEAMS

An airport's landing beams make a pink cross appear on the primary flight display's artificial horizon. Using the control column, you line the white bars up with the pink cross to make the plane stay on course.

CHOCS AWAY!

When a plane has come to a halt, blocks called *chocs* are put in front of the wheels. They stop the plane from rolling. The chocs must be removed before the plane can take off — chocs away!

41

You can qualify as an airline pilot in several ways. Whichever route you take, you must:

- be at least 21 years old
- hold the full Air Transport Pilot Licence (ATPL)
- have good educational qualifications (at least two high grade A-levels in maths and physics and often a degree)
- have good coordination, eyesight and physical fitness.

It's also really useful to gain pre-entry experience and show your interest by joining the Air Training Corps (ATC). Also experience of challenging activities like Duke of Edinburgh's Award or community work is very valuable.

Steps to becoming a commercial pilot

Good grades in maths and physics are a must!

Get as much flying experience as you can.

DIDYOUKNOW?

Many airlines will expect you to pay for your own 'type training' to qualify to fly certain aircrafts, or pay the airline a bond of £15,000 to £30,000 to cover part of your training. Your bond will be repaid to you over several years if you stay with that airline.

There are four routes:

1. *University* – several UK universities offer courses in air transport and operations with pilot training options. Some of these allow you to study to 'frozen' ATPL level but you may have to fund the flight training modules yourself. See the UCAS website for more details.

2. *Private training schools* – you can fund your own training at a CAA approved training school but the full cost would be around £60,000 for the 700 hours minimum flying hours required.

3. *Sponsored training* – some airlines offer sponsorships for those with A-levels / Higher levels in maths and physics but entry requirements vary. BALPA and the Air League have details of airline sponsorships, bursaries and scholarships (see page 45).

4. *Armed Forces experience* – many qualified pilots from the forces eventually move to airlines. They need to do a conversion course. There is strong competition for pilot training in the forces and you must serve a minimum term before taking up employment with an airline.

Other related career areas to consider:

APART FROM THE NATIONAL AND COMMUTER AIRLINES, OTHER FLYING OPPORTUNITIES EXIST FOR:

- FLYING INSTRUCTORS
- CROP SPRAYING
- FREELANCE CHARTER SERVICES

RELATED JOBS INCLUDE:

- AIR CABIN CREW
- AIR TRAFFIC CONTROLLERS
- RAF NON-COMMISSIONED AIRCREW
- HELICOPTER PILOT
- RAF OR ROYAL NAVY OFFICER
- AEROSPACE ENGINEER

In addition to major airline companies, commercial pilots can also find employment with:
- government agencies, e.g. the police, customs, coast watch, forest and national parks
- aerial surveying services, e.g. aerial photography and mapping to monitor environmental changes and civil engineering projects
- aeromedical services, e.g. services that fly doctors and/or nurses to remote areas where people need medical care
- aircraft sales companies.

Useful contacts

Connexions / Careers Service and UCAS www.ucas.ac.uk
For details of university degree courses, ask your Connexions / Careers Service or look at the UCAS website.

Air Training Corps (ATC) www.aircadets.org
Gain some aviation experience by joining the Air Training Corps.

The Civil Aviation Authority (CAA) www.caa.co.uk
The CAA approve training schools. Details of approved training schools can be found on their website.

British Airline Pilots Association (BALPA) www.balpa.org
Balpa House, 5 Heathrow Boulevard, 278 Bath Road, West Drayton UB7 0DQ
BALPA provide general details about airline pilot careers.

The British Women Pilots' Association (BWPA) www.bwpa.co.uk
Brooklands Museum, Brooklands Road, Weybridge, Surrey KT13 0QN

British Airways www.britishairwaysjobs.com/baweb1/
The Rivers, Cranebank, Silver Junilee Way, Cranford, Middlesex Tel: 0870 608 0747

Royal Aeronautical Society (RAE) www.raes.org.uk
RAE give details of vacancies and possible employers.

Further information

For details of scholarships which may cover part of the training cost contact:
The Air League www.airleague.co.uk
British Airline Pilots Association (BALPA) www.balpa.org

See these magazines and websites for job opportunities:
Pilot Magazine www.pilotweb.aero
Professional Pilots' Job Network www.ppjn.com

Glossary

aeronautical – relating to aircraft or their flight

aviation – the design, manufacture and use of aircraft

beacon – a radio transmitter that broadcasts a signal to guide aircraft

civilian – a person who is not in the armed forces

commercial – something that's used to make money

domestic – occurring within a country

forerunner – somebody or something that has a function similar to somebody or something coming later

frontal system – where one mass of air meets another that is different in temperature or density

gyroscopes – a self-stabilising device; a rotating heavy metal wheel inside a circular frame; lets the wheel's axis keep its original direction even though the frame is moved around; used in compasses and other navigational aids

jet stream – a strong high-altitude wind current

navigate – to work out the direction you should travel; sometimes using maps or instruments

phonetic – relating to the sounds of human speech

pitch – to move in a rolling front-to-rear motion

Rolls Royce Trent – a family of jet engines manufactured by the Rolls Royce company

supersonic – moving faster than the speed of sound

theories – ideas that are meant to explain something